Mary D. Lankford

Christmas
Around the World

Illustrated by Karen Dugan

Morrow Junior Books   New York

1. Australia
2. Canada
3. Ethiopia
4. Germany
5. Great Britain
6. Greece
7. Guatemala
8. Italy
9. Mexico
10. The Philippines
11. Sweden
12. United States—Alaska

*For Beverly Braun, Carlyn Gray, Julie Judd, and
Sue Rose, friends and librarians who have given me
their greatest gifts: time, laughter, and love*
—M.D.L.

With love to Rose Merenda
—K.D.

ACKNOWLEDGMENTS

Writing this book was like gathering threads to make a beautiful Christmas tapestry. I drew information from friends in different countries, from interviews and books, from newspaper and magazine articles, and from government publications whose authors I will never know.

A special note of appreciation to Mary Frank and Jim Haupt in Nuremberg, Germany, for providing information on German customs; Leonard and Marge McCown and Rosemary and Carl Johnson for Sweden; Molly Bynum for Alaska and also Jeff Lear and Helen M. Howard of the Alaskan Native Language Center, University of Alaska, Fairbanks; Joni Treadaway for Guatemala; Hamelmal Teffera for Ethiopia; and Eva Katsari for Greece. Thanks to the staff of the children's department at Irving Public Library: Julie Judd, Laurie Chase, Joanne Sherlock, Elaine Markley; also to the librarians of the Irving Independent School District who provided many resources; and finally, to Karla Munroe for her continued support and encouragement.

I sorted through these threads, discarded some, and wove the rest into patterns of custom, tradition, geography, and history to describe Christmas celebrations around the world today.

Contents

Ideas, and a Christmas Wish

The question frequently asked of an author is "Where do you get your ideas?" The idea for this book came from my editor, who suggested that Christmas might be a good subject for a companion volume to *Hopscotch Around the World.* My initial reaction was negative. I felt that the many Christmas books published each year provided enough information on the subject. I reluctantly started my research and was surprised to find how few books gave information about customs in countries other than the United States. As I continued my research, I was amazed by the richness of the Christmas heritage. Slowly, gathering information from many sources, I began to think of the traditions of Christmas as a beautifully decorated Christmas tree. Its roots were the pagan rites heralding the end of winter and the promise of spring. These pagan beliefs were then absorbed into Christian rituals as the celebration of the Christ Child's birth grew and spread like the boughs of a magnificent fir.

I discovered that there are similarities and intriguing differences in the way Christmas is celebrated from continent to continent. It was because of this splendid diversity that I finally agreed there *was* merit in a book about Christmas customs around the world. I wanted the reader to appreciate the geographical uniqueness of each country, as well as the range of customs celebrated there. Above all, I wanted to interest the reader in learning more.

I had a difficult task in choosing only twelve countries and then limiting my text to a sampling of customs from each one. I hope readers will be inspired to seek additional information from grandparents who still remember holiday customs in the "old country" and from relatives and friends more recently arrived from the nations of their births.

People have come to North America from all the countries in this book. Some of my most satisfying research was done right in my home state of Texas. Interviews provided fascinating glimpses of family traditions that have been lovingly maintained. And I have been fortunate, in recent years, to join Christmas celebrations in England, Scandinavia, and Germany. The wealth of library resources, filmstrips, magazines, books (cookbooks were a surprisingly rich source), and newspapers made my decision about what information to include even more difficult.

As readers "sample" each country, they will find its customs are like reflective Christmas ornaments hanging on a fir tree. Customs echo the unique beauty of all cultures and the strengths of similar beliefs shared by many people. To expand the scope of the text, I added a glossary of Christmas facts and fiction, and a time line of important dates. I hope that the craft section will encourage readers to use their imaginations and adapt some of the wonderful customs I discovered to their own resources and experience.

Just as there are many ways to celebrate Christmas, there are differences of opinion about the date of Christ's birth. Although December 25 may not be exactly right, the spirit of the celebration is more important than the actual date. I hope this book will serve as a reminder that the birth of *any* child creates memories that will be forever wrapped in feelings of anticipation, excitement, surprise, and delight. Celebration of the birth of the Christ Child reminds us that throughout the year we should fill our hearts with the spirit of kindness, generosity, and love. May December 25 become a day we acknowledge that by giving to others, we create joy that will remain in our hearts long after the Christmas season ends.

A Christmas Chronology

6 B.C. Approximate date for birth of Jesus Christ

A.D. 280 Approximate birth date of St. Nicholas

320 Pope Julius I, bishop of Rome, proclaims December 25 the official celebration date for birthday of Christ.

567 Council of Tours establishes Advent as a period of fasting and the time between Christmas and Epiphany as a sacred, festive season.

1492 Christopher Columbus's ship *Santa María* is wrecked on island of Hispaniola in the Caribbean Sea on Christmas Eve. Colony is named La Navidad in honor of the day.

1561 First printed reference to Christmas trees, in Germany

1643 British Parliament officially abolishes celebration of Christmas.

1818 "Silent Night" is written on Christmas Eve, in Obendorf, Austria.

1822 Dr. Clement Moore writes "A Visit from St. Nicholas," better known by its first line, "'Twas the night before Christmas."

1836 Alabama is the first state to declare Christmas a legal holiday.

1843 First Christmas card is printed, in England.

1843 Charles Dickens writes *A Christmas Carol.*

1856 President Franklin Pierce decorates first White House Christmas tree.

1857 "Jingle Bells" is written by J. Pierpont.

1890 Oklahoma, which became a state in 1907, is the last territory to declare Christmas a legal holiday.

1926 United States dedicates the Nation's Christmas Tree, a giant sequoia, in Kings Canyon National Park, California.

1937 First postage stamp to commemorate Christmas is issued, in Austria.

1949 "Rudolph the Red-Nosed Reindeer" is recorded by Gene Autry.

1962 First Christmas postage stamp is issued in the United States.

Australia

SYMBOL: *Candlelight*
GREETING: *Merry Christmas*
WEATHER: *Sizzling heat*

Early maps called Australia *terra australis incognita*, or the unknown southern land. Although Aborigines had lived there for forty thousand years, in 1770 Captain James Cook claimed the land for Great Britain and renamed it New South Wales. The continent of Australia is almost equal in size to the United States and is the sixth largest country in the world. The six colonies established by early settlers are now called states. One of its external territories, Christmas Island, was named by Captain William Mynors of the British East India Company on Christmas Day, 1643.

Many Christmas customs were brought by early settlers from England. However, the celebrations in damp, cold England were bound to change on an island continent that lies well below the equator. Australian Christmas cards sometimes picture the many unique animals found on this continent. Kangaroos, koalas, and wombats appear with unusual plants such as the eucalyptus, a native tree of Australia, and the baobab, often described as an upside-down tree.

Although Christmas falls during the summer vacation, crowds fill the churches for special services on Christmas Eve and Christmas Day. After a grand breakfast of ham fried with eggs, some families follow church services with a picnic at the beach.

The traditional turkey dinner sometimes ends with a flaming Christmas plum pudding for dessert. Made with suet, or meat fat, spices, raisins, and apples (but no plums), it is steamed for six hours. In the days of the Australian gold rush, Christmas puddings frequently contained gold nuggets. Today a coin or small favor is baked inside, and whoever finds it knows to expect good luck.

Homes may be decorated with ferns, palm leaves, the red and green flowering Christmas bush, and the yellow-edged, bell-shaped Christmas bell flower. Other flowers blooming in December include nasturtiums, wisteria, and honeysuckle. Children can search for the gold Christmas beetle. This small clumsy insect appears around Christmastime and flies into windows or clings to clothes.

Australian children are told that Father Christmas or, sometimes, Santa Claus will leave gifts for them on Christmas Eve. Costumed representatives of these two gift givers may be shown arriving by helicopter or boat in parades marking the beginning of the Christmas season. Gifts are sometimes tucked into the pillowcases on children's beds, or found at the breakfast table.

Since 1937 many Australians have made Carols by Candlelight part of their Christmas tradition. The custom began when a radio announcer, Norman Banks, noticed an old woman sitting alone at her window, listening by candlelight to Christmas carols on her radio. The following Christmas, Banks launched his idea for an annual community singing event in the city of Melbourne. The idea spread to other cities. Shops sell special candles for this event and donate all proceeds to charities. As darkness falls in the late-summer evening, candles are lit by members of the choir, dressed in white. Overhead, the sky is decorated with stars, some of which form the Southern Cross constellation. Parks are filled with audiences holding flickering candles, listening to the choir members, and blending their voices as they sing Christmas carols. The program concludes with "Auld Lang Syne," sung at midnight.

Canada

Canada, the largest country in the world, claims 7 percent of the earth's surface, or almost four million square miles. Its ten provinces and two territories sweep across the North American continent from Newfoundland on the Atlantic Ocean to British Columbia on the Pacific Ocean.

Sixteenth-century French explorers first opened Canada's rich territories for fur traders and later for colonists from Europe. They established a French stronghold that survived decades of bitter struggle with the British in the seventeenth and eighteenth centuries. The province of Quebec retained its French language and customs, which is why the two official languages of Canada today are English and French.

Canada and the United States share a border of 5,527 miles. Both countries continue to welcome new citizens from around the world. More than 4,600,000 immigrants have entered Canada since the conclusion of World War II. Immigrants bring a rich heritage of Christmas customs and family traditions to their new homes. Christmas trees, Santa Claus, stockings hung by the chimney, and colorful outside lights are familiar sights in both Canada and the United States.

In Nova Scotia, during the twelve days of Christmas, small groups of *belsnicklers,* or masked mummers, appear in neighborhoods, ringing bells, making noise, seeking candy or other treats. Their host may provide Christmas cake or a drink made from a mixture of water and thick, sweet syrup. Costumes may include Grandma's nightgown or Dad's winter underwear. The host attempts to identify the disguised visitors. Once identified, the mummer removes his or her mask and ceases making noises and rude actions. Children in the house may be quizzed by the belsnicklers about their behavior. If the children reply that they have been good, they are rewarded with candy.

The French-speaking Canadians of Quebec display crèches, or Nativity scenes, in their homes as part of their Christmas decoration. After attending midnight mass, families may be served *tourtière,* or pork pie. Another favorite food is *boulettes,* or small meatballs. A Christmas banquet is called a *réveillon.* Banquets for reunions of extended families require months of planning. Many family groups include thirty or forty relatives.

In British Columbia, Christmas turkey may be accompanied by either fresh or smoked salmon. People of British heritage may serve brussels sprouts, mincemeat pie, or trifle and will place a decorative favor, called a Christmas cracker, at each plate. Whimsical paper hats found in the cracker are worn during dinner.

A flotilla, or parade of ships, is organized in Vancouver Harbor in the two weeks prior to Christmas. Carols ring out across the water as children's choirs on the ships echo the sound of ringing bells. Onshore spectators view a harbor filled with ships silhouetted in lights, their mastheads decorated with Christmas trees.

The *aurora borealis,* or northern lights, casts an eerie green curtain of lights over the forests of fir trees. Trees are grown as an export crop in different parts of Canada. From October through the first day of December, Christmas trees are baled and loaded, sixteen hundred per truck, for a journey of thousands of miles to the United States. Some are also sent by ship to South America. They bring the joy of Christmas and a part of Canada into many homes.

Ethiopia

SYMBOL: *Fringed, beautifully embroidered umbrella*
GREETING: Melkm Ganna, *or Good Christmas*
WEATHER: *Rainfall and temperature range from cool moist mountain air to scorching heat along the border*

Ethiopia, which forms part of the horn of Africa, has always been a symbol of independence for the African continent. Unlike many of its neighbors, it was never a European colony. Its capital, Addis Ababa, is close to the exact geographical center of the country and has a wonderfully musical name that means new flower. In the ancient Egyptian world, the word *ethiopia* meant all lands south of Egypt, and the country that is now Ethiopia was called *Punt,* or the land of God. Egyptian ships sailed to Ethiopia to purchase spices, incense, and myrrh.

In the Ethiopian Coptic church, *Ganna,* or Christmas, is celebrated on January 7. This celebration takes place in Ethiopia's ancient rectangular churches carved, over 800 years ago, from solid volcanic rock and in modern round churches that are designed in three concentric circles. Men and boys sit separately from girls and women. The choir sings from the outside circle. The second circle, or holy place, is for the congregation. Holy Communion is served in the innermost circle, the sanctuary. Following a day of fasting, everyone attending the early-morning mass wears white. People receive candles as they enter the church. After lighting the candles everyone walks around the church three times, then stands throughout the mass, which may last up to three hours.

Ganna is also the name of a game played only on this day by Ethiopian boys. Similar to hockey, ganna is played with a stick and wooden puck. Players frequently endure cuts and broken bones in the rough-and-tumble action. At nightfall the game ends as the teams shout naughty limericks at each other.

Timkat, a three-day holiday unique to Ethiopia, starts on January 19 and celebrates the baptism of Christ. A newly washed *shamma,* or rectangular shawl, is worn by adults to the church services. Children walk in a festive procession, wearing crowns and robes identified with particular church youth groups. Priests, dressed in red-and-white robes, wear turbans and carry beautifully embroidered umbrellas. Music for the ceremony may be that of the *sistrum,* a rattlelike percussion instrument shaped like a spade or pear. The sistrum has small metal disks that make a tinkling sound when shaken. The beat is tapped out by the *makamiya,* or prayer stick. This long pole is T-shaped and is also used as a support for the clergy during lengthy services. The *meleket,* or Ethiopian musical chant, is learned by *dabtaras,* or church officials, after rigorous study. Dabtaras are trained in theology and have an important part in church affairs.

During Timkat Ethiopians play a sport called *yeferas guks.* In a large field, teams pursue one another on horseback, throwing ceremonial lances. Young men on the teams, dressed in white, wear lion-mane capes and headdresses. Hippopotamus hides are used as shields.

Christmas food in Ethiopia usually includes *injerá,* a sourdough pancakelike bread that can be easily cooked over an open fire. Injerá serves as both plate and fork. *Doro wat,* a spicy chicken stew, might be the main dish for dinner. A piece of the injerá is used to scoop up a portion of wat. Beautifully designed basketlike stands are used to serve the wat.

An Ethiopian child would be amazed to see the many Christmas gifts received by children in other parts of the world. Gift giving is a very small part of their Christmas celebration. Children usually receive very simple presents like a small gift of clothing.

Germany

SYMBOL: Tannenbaum, *or Christmas tree*
GREETING: Fröhliche Weihnachten, *or Merry Christmas*
WEATHER: *Mild and damp to very cold and bright; there are always some* weisse wochen, *or white weeks*

Can you think of another nation like Germany that shares its border with nine other countries? German people live by the sea in the north and in Alpine mountains to the south. Berlin, the capital, is the largest city in Europe.

Germany is famous for its Christmas markets. Nuremberg's *Christkindlesmarkt,* or Christ Child Market, is the oldest and most famous in Germany. From early December to Christmas Eve, the winter air is filled with the aroma of baked fruit loaves; *bratwurst,* or sausage; roasted nuts; and *lebkuchen,* a spicy cookie. The recipe for lebkuchen is a treasured secret and includes nuts, eggs, honey, sugar, flour, and cardamom, clove, cinnamon, and coriander. The spices represent a time when Nuremberg was a center for the spice trade. Nuremberg shoppers make their way between the red-roofed stalls, purchasing food, toys, Christmas decorations, and *Zwetschgenmännla* and *Zwetschgenfrauen,* or prune men and prune women.

These unique figures, about ten inches high, have arms and legs made of prunes threaded over wire, dried figs for bodies, and walnut heads painted with expressive faces. These traditional folk figures are costumed as musicians, farmers, chimney sweeps …the choices are endless. A sign over one of the stalls selling the Zwetschgenmännla offers this advice: "You will never be without gold and happiness, if you have a prune person in your house."

City streets leading to the outdoor market are decorated with greenery and with Nuremberg angels. Dressed in stiff, accordion-pleated paper dresses, the angels are the symbol for Nuremberg and represent the star followed by the Wise Men.

In rural Bavaria, the three Thursday evenings before Christmas are called *Klöpfelnachten,* or knocking nights. On a Klöpfelnacht, masked children travel through the neighborhood, clanging cowbells and banging lids. They knock on their neighbors' doors and recite a rhyme that begins with the word *knock.* Their neighbors, in turn, give them candy, coins, or fruit.

German children also ask for presents by writing a letter to the Christ Child. They put glue on the envelope and sprinkle it with sugar so it will glisten when left on a windowsill. Another tradition is to fill shoes with straw and carrots and leave them outside the front door. It is hoped that when St. Nicholas passes by, he will feed his hungry horse and refill the shoes of good children with apples and nuts. Children who have misbehaved find their shoes filled with sticks or coal.

The idea of decorating a Christmas tree may have originated in Germany. There are many legends about the very first tree. One tale describes how a woodcutter befriends a small hungry child. The next morning, the child appears to the woodcutter and his wife and identifies himself as the *Christkindlein,* or little Christ Child. He breaks a branch from a fir tree and explains to the couple that at Christmastime the tree will always bear fruit. Every year thereafter, the tree blossoms with apples of gold and nuts of silver.

In another legend, Martin Luther, a German minister and reformer, decorated a fir tree with candles and brought it into his home. The candle-lit tree symbolized the light of Christ.

Decorations for Christmas trees have changed over the years. In the 1600s, branches were hung with paper roses, cookies, and fruit. Now they are decorated with beautiful glass ornaments of many shapes and sizes, cornucopias, wooden angels, straw stars, and lebkuchen baked in different shapes. The factory workers, craftspeople, and

wood-carvers of Germany have created many of the ornaments and decorations that are treasured around the world.

Heiligabend, or Christmas Eve, is said to be a magical time when the pure in heart can hear animals talking. Adults gather in each household to decorate the Christmas tree. Just after dark a bell rings, and finally the children are allowed to view the lighted tree with presents piled underneath waiting to be opened.

Great Britain

SYMBOL: *Christmas crackers*
GREETING: *Merry Christmas*
WEATHER: *Usually damp, foggy, and cold*

Great Britain, one of the British Isles, includes England, Wales, and Scotland. Great Britain and Northern Ireland together form the United Kingdom. In 1643 the celebration of Christmas was outlawed by English Puritans because they thought it was too closely tied to pagan beliefs. The holiday was reestablished as a celebration in 1660.

Many elements of the Christmas celebration are tied to ancient beliefs. Present-day shop windows and homes are brightened by green leaves and bright red berries of the holly tree, sprigs of ivy, and mistletoe. The Druids, a pagan priesthood, considered holly, ivy, and mistletoe to be magical because they remained green throughout the winter.

Queen Victoria ruled England from 1837 to 1901. The custom of decorating Christmas trees was made popular by her husband, Prince Albert, who brought the idea from his native Germany. The Victorian candle-lit trees were decorated with fruit, nuts, candy, and roses.

In the 1840s the first Christmas card was designed by English artist John Calcott Horsley. Something like a modern postcard, it pictured a large family enjoying Christmas. In 1870 lower postage rates and less expensive reproduction made exchanging Christmas cards a popular custom.

In 1844 Thomas Smith, an English candy maker, visited France and saw *cosaques*, or crackers, sugar-coated almonds wrapped in squares of colored paper that were twisted at each end. He returned to England and began making crackers that contained candy, mottoes, jokes, and riddles. By the turn of the century Thomas Smith's firm was selling 13 million crackers each year. Today's cracker is a crepe-paper-covered tube with small trinkets inside. At Christmas dinner a cracker is placed beside each plate, and when its end tabs are pulled, a chemically treated paper strip breaks and makes a popping or cracking noise.

In the 1600s colonists in North America sent the first turkeys to Britain. Christmas Day dinner may now include turkeys raised in England, but cranberry sauce must still be imported from the United States. Serving plum pudding, or Christmas pudding, is a tradition that the British took with them to many countries they explored and colonized. A foil-wrapped coin baked in the plum pudding batter is said to bring good luck.

The first person to visit a home on Christmas Day sometimes shouts, "First footing." Good luck comes to the house if this first guest brings a gift. Following Christmas dinner most families listen to the annual radio and television message from the monarch. After Christmas, families sometimes make a leftover dish called "bubble and squeak." This fried crisp cake is a combination of mashed potatoes and brussels sprouts from the Christmas Day meal.

Boxing Day, celebrated on December 26, is uniquely British. It has nothing to do with fighting. Originally, on this public holiday, church alms boxes, filled with donations for the poor, were opened and the money distributed. Now people often give gifts of money to servants or other people who have given service during the year, such as postal workers, newspaper vendors, or police.

Boxing Day also marks the beginning of the Christmas pantomimes. This activity originally meant a play without words, or an actor who mimed or entertained without speaking. Pantomime now refers to all kinds of plays performed during the Christmas season. Children's stories such as "Jack and the Bean Stalk" and "Cinderella" are often performed.

Greece

Symbol: Christopsomo, *or Christ bread*
Greeting: Kala Christougena, *or Merry Christmas*
Weather: *Western Mediterranean winds cause mild temperatures, heavy rainfall throughout the winter months*

If it were possible to throw a *drachma*, a Greek coin, as far as eighty miles, you could make this toss from any place in Greece and hit one of the seas that surround the country. Because Greece has over 9,385 miles of coastline there are many opportunities to make a living from the sea. In Greece, St. Nicholas, a giver of gifts during the Christmas season, is also the patron saint of sailors and fishermen. Legends surround the life of this saint, who was the bishop of the city of Myra, an ancient city in Asia Minor, at the beginning of the fourth century. At Christmas, to honor St. Nicholas, many small fishing boats are decorated with blue and white lights—these are also the colors of the Greek flag.

Merry Christmas written in Greek looks like this:

Καλά Χριστούγεννα

There are only twenty-four letters in the Greek alphabet, and some are very different in shape from our roman letters.

Most Greek homes trim an evergreen tree with tinsel and top it with a star. Gifts are exchanged on January 1, St. Basil's Day. St. Basil, one of the four Fathers of the Greek Orthodox church, is supposed to visit all Greek homes on the first day of the year. Some families leave a log in the fireplace for St. Basil to step on as he climbs down the chimney with toys.

On Christmas Eve, large groups of friends and family gather around the holiday table. Figs, dried

on flat rooftops in summer sun, are served with the spicy, golden *Christopsomo* bread. These large sweet loaves are often decorated with a frosted ornament representing family interests or occupation (such as a plow for a farm family), or sometimes with a cross. Dried fruit, nuts, and honey are also served. Before the meal begins, the sign of the cross is made over the bread, and the table is lifted three times.

Christmas morning usually begins with a seven o'clock mass in the Greek Orthodox church. After church, groups of boys and girls go from house to house, singing carols. They are rewarded with something sweet to eat or a small gift. The word *carol* comes from the Greek word *choraulein*, a combination of *choros*, or dance, and *aulein*, to play the flute. Others may accompany these carolers on musical instruments such as triangles or clay drums.

As family and friends arrive for the Christmas Day feast they may greet one another by saying, *"Hronia polla,"* or "Many happy years." The extended family gathering may include many aunts, uncles, cousins, and grandparents. The food-filled table may have roast turkey stuffed with chestnuts, rice, or pine nuts, served with a variety of vegetables. Sweet dishes may include *kourambiethes,* a Greek nut cookie. These cookies each have a whole clove stuck in them as a symbol of the spices brought to Jesus by the Three Wise Men. *Baklava,* another sweet Greek dessert, is made from layers of phyllo pastry, filled with almonds and cinnamon, and soaked in lemon syrup.

Celebrations conclude on Epiphany, or Greek Cross Day. (Epiphany falls on January 6, the day the Three Wise Men were said to have reached Bethlehem.) On this day, crucifixes are given the Blessing of the Waters by being dipped into the sea or a river by a priest. Once people believed that on this day animals could talk and wishes would be granted.

Guatemala

SYMBOL: Tres Reyes, *or Three Kings*
GREETING: Feliz Navidad, *or Happy Nativity*
WEATHER: *Dry, with springlike temperatures in the mountains, hot and humid near the coast*

Guatemala is primarily agricultural, but it has many beautiful mountainous areas and shares a heritage with other Central American countries that began in ancient Indian civilizations. Almost half of the people of Guatemala are descendants of the Maya Quiche Indians. The creative heritage of the Maya Quiche is shown through ancient weaving methods still used to create unique patterns and designs in clothing worn today. Each village has its own brilliant colors, dress design, and fabric patterns.

Guatemala's interior is divided by a range of about thirty massive volcanic cones. Mountain forests provide a background for some of the 1,200 species of orchids. The ancient Maya probably used the vanilla orchid as a flavor to enhance warm chocolate drinks. Christmas begins during the dry season, when flowers and fruits are abundant.

The Spanish conquered and converted the Maya to Christianity over 400 years ago. Mayan descendants accepted the Christian beliefs, but many of their ancient rituals were adapted to Catholic ceremonies. An example is the *Palo Voladare*, or flying pole dance, an unusual celebration that takes place on St. Thomas Day, December 21. One of Jesus's twelve Apostles, St. Thomas is the patron saint of the town of Chichicastenango. There, by performing the Palo Voladare, descendants of the Maya also honor the sun god they worshiped long before they became Christians. Three men climb to a platform at the top of a fifty-foot pole. Long ropes have been attached to the pole. Two of the men take a rope each and wind it around their ankles. As they jump from the platform, the ropes unwind and the two dancers slowly descend to the ground. It is believed that if the men land on their feet, the sun god will be pleased, and each day the hours of light will grow longer.

Daily, throughout the Christmas season, several religious statues are taken for an elaborate procession. They are carried on crimson-canopied litters hung with peacock or ostrich feathers, mirrors, tinsel, and paper flowers. At the rear of this parade of popular saints is an image representing God Himself. This white-bearded figure may resemble a department-store Santa Claus. Marimbas and *chirimias* accompany the marchers throughout the procession until the images are returned to the church. On Christmas Eve festivities conclude at midnight with a *Misa de Gallo*, or Mass of the Rooster. Usually this mass is held early in the morning, when roosters traditionally sound their call to awake. But at Christmas the Misa de Gallo honors the legend of a rooster that crowed at midnight, the moment Christ was born. Current-day roosters must certainly be wakened by the fireworks, whistle blowing, and bell ringing that follow the mass!

Nacimientos, or manger scenes, are displayed in churches and public places. In homes, small figures are added to the nacimiento each year so that an entire room may eventually be used for the scene. The figure of the Christ Child is added on Christmas Eve.

In most Central American countries Epiphany is called *el Dia de los Reyes*, or the Day of the Kings, or sometimes, Twelfth Day. This festival is primarily a children's holiday. For weeks prior to Epiphany, children write letters to the Three Kings. On the evening of January 5, children place their shoes on their balcony or in front of their door. Some children also leave a little hay and water for the Wise Men's camels. The next morning toys and candy fill the shoes.

Italy

Symbol: Presepio, *or manger scene*
Greeting: Buon Natale, *or Good Christmas*
Weather: *Ranges from the cold and snow of the northern mountains to the warmth of the southern Mediterranean coast*

Italy is a boot-shaped peninsula that stretches from its borders with France, Switzerland, Austria, and Yugoslavia to the island of Sicily in the Mediterranean Sea. A trip from the top of the boot to its "toe" takes over twenty-four hours by train.

The sounds of Christmas traditionally include music from the *zampognari*, or itinerant bagpipers, who travel from mountain villages dressed in sheepskin jackets with thong-laced stockings. These mountain men look as if they have just arrived from the original manger scene. Moving from house to house, they play hymns as they stand before the *presepio*.

The word *presepio* comes from the Latin word *praesaepe*, meaning enclosure, crib, or manger. Throughout the Christmas season hundreds of different presepi, or manger scenes, are displayed. In large cathedrals, visitors view life-size scenes that may include animated figures of horses, camels, and everyday people who might have had an opportunity to bring a gift to the Christ Child. In their homes, families carefully unwrap presepi that are treasures handed down through generations. Some families have a tradition of gathering before the manger scene each evening during the nine days before Christmas—the time it is said to have taken Mary and Joseph to make the journey to Bethlehem. Candles are lighted and prayers are given. This custom may have originated with St. Francis of Assisi over seven hundred years ago.

The *ceppo*, or Christmas pyramid, is often displayed during the holiday season. This decoration has three or four shelves on which puppets, pinecones, flags, and figurines of angels are placed. The

bottom shelf may contain the presepio. Small gifts of candy or toys may also be added to the ceppo. Some stores sell ceppi already decorated.

In another Italian tradition, children write letters to their parents, extending wishes for a wonderful Christmas celebration and including promises that misbehavior will cease. These letters are read aloud at the dinner table and then are allowed to float up the chimney in the heat of a crackling fire. As they watch their wishes disappear, the children chant these words to the mythical character Befana:

> *Befana, Befana,*
> *You are my lady,*
> *You are my wife.*
> *Throw something down to me—*
> *A little orange or a* pefanino
> *Or a small piece of* pecorino.

The pefanino is a small cookie shaped like Befana. Pecorino is a special kind of cheese.

Befana was an old witch woman who refused to go with the Three Kings to Bethlehem because she was too busy sweeping her house. After completing her work, she set out to find the Christ Child but lost her way. The legend says that she continues her search for Baby Jesus, and on January 5, the night before Epiphany, Italian children leave their shoes by the fireplace, hoping that Befana will slip down the chimney on her broomstick and leave gifts for them.

Italian children don't have to wait until January 6 to receive all their presents. They also expect gifts on Christmas Day. Some believe that the gifts come from *Bambino Gesù*, or Baby Jesus; others count on *Babbo Natale*, or Father Christmas.

Christmas Eve dinner in an Italian home may include a baked eel, which may be four feet long. Pasta will certainly be found in one of its many shapes. A capon or small chicken stuffed with a chestnut dressing is another option for Christmas dinner. *Panettone*, a loaf-shaped Christmas cake, is made with raisins and citron.

At noon on Christmas Day, the pope, leader of the Roman Catholic Church, gives his blessing to crowds gathered in the huge Vatican square.

Mexico

Symbol: Flor de la noche buena, *or flower of the Nativity*
Greeting: Feliz Navidad, *or Happy Nativity*
Weather: *During mild, warm days and cool nights, blooming flowers scent the air*

Bound on the east by the Gulf of Mexico and the west by the Pacific Ocean, Mexico is beautiful and mountainous. It was given its name by the Aztecs, the Indian people who once ruled the country. The first Mexican Christmas was celebrated in 1538 by missionaries from Spain.

Beginning on December 16, children take part in *las posadas*, a daily reenactment of Mary and Joseph's journey to Bethlehem. Led by two children carrying small statues of Mary and Joseph, a procession of friends and neighbors goes from house to house, seeking *posada*, or shelter. When they find a homeowner who will invite them inside, those in the procession place the figures of Mary and Joseph in the *nacimiento*, or manger scene, that is found in all homes. The pageant, using the same children, is reenacted until Christmas Eve. On the last posada evening, children go to the church to place a figure of the Christ Child in the nacimiento there. Members of the procession and their families and friends remain in the church to attend midnight mass.

Each day from December 16 until Christmas Eve, the posada ceremony is followed by a feast at one of the participants' homes. Often children attempt to break a *piñata*. The piñata, a papier-mâché figure, may be shaped like a star, a flower, an animal, a bird, or a house. It can be raised to and lowered from the ceiling, and when it is broken, candy or small gifts scatter on the floor.

Families shop for gifts or decorations at *puestos*, or market stalls, in the Christmas markets that spring up during the holiday season. The Mexican flag, with its broad red, white, and green stripes, can be seen everywhere as a part of the Christmas decorations.

The days leading to Christmas are filled with the wonderful smell of *buñuelos*, thin round pastries covered with sugar and cinnamon. Christmas dinner may include *ensalada de la noche buena*, a fruit-and-vegetable mixture; roast turkey (which sixteenth-century explorer Hernando Cortés took back to Spain from Mexico); tortillas; and hot chocolate with vanilla and cinnamon. A special Christmas salad, *ensalada navideña*, includes fruit, beets, sugarcane, and nuts and is decorated with small colored candies.

On Epiphany eve children place their shoes in a window of their homes. The next morning their shoes are filled with gifts given by the *Reyes Magos*, or Magi, on their journey to Bethlehem.

Adding to the colors of this festive time of year is the *flor de la noche buena*, which is admired for its flame-colored leaves. In the United States it is called the poinsettia plant, named for Joel Robert Poinsett, who served as American ambassador to Mexico from 1825 to 1829.

In Oaxaca, a city 340 miles southeast of Mexico City, December 23 is *la Noche de los Rábanos*, or the Night of the Radishes. In 1897 a contest was held to encourage farmers to grow bigger and better vegetables for the December 23 market, the biggest market day of the year. They were judged on how cleverly they could carve radishes! Today the carved figures may represent religious scenes, animals, folktale characters, or spaceships. Their sizes range from a few inches to one or two feet. The root of the radish may be used as part of the figure or serve as an arm or leg. The figures are still judged and prizes awarded.

The holiday season officially ends on February 2 with a religious service called *el Dia de la Candelaria*, or Candlemas. Candles are used in the ceremony, which celebrates a passage from the Bible. In Luke 2:22–38, Mary follows tradition by taking Jesus to the Temple in Jerusalem and presenting Him as her firstborn. An elderly man named Simeon recognizes the infant as "A light to lighten the Gentiles and the glory of thy people Israel." This is one of the many images of light used in the Bible to describe Jesus.

The Philippines

SYMBOL: Parol, *or Christmas star*
GREETING: Maligayang Pasko, *or Merry Christmas*
WEATHER: *Warm and humid*

This archipelago, an independent republic, includes over seven thousand islands. If all the islands were pushed together, they would form one land mass about the size of Arizona.

The Philippines is the only Asian nation in which Christianity is the religion of choice of most of the people. Christmas celebrations often begin nine days before Christmas with a *Misa de Gallo* similar to the Mass of the Rooster celebrated in Guatemala. At the mass, the story of the birth of Christ is read from the Bible. The following days are filled with the sound of firecrackers; the sight of thousands of *parols*, or star lanterns; and the smell of fruit drinks and *puto bumbong*, a special steamed rice.

The *Panunuluyan* pageant is held each Christmas Eve. A couple is chosen to reenact Joseph and Mary's search for shelter. Dressed in costume, they stop at many doors, knock, and are then joined by the people inside. Their destination is the church, which they know will finally give them shelter. Members of the procession carry parols to light their way.

Mass is held hourly on Christmas Day so that everyone can attend. Many religious services include a *pastore*, or play, based on the story of the birth of the Christ Child. The pastore closes with a star from the upper part of the church sliding down a wire and coming to rest over the church's Nativity scene.

Parols, placed in the windows of homes and apartments, may be found in all sizes. Some communities have contests to decide which star lantern is the most beautiful or the largest. Many parols have a large *rolyo*, or ring, around the outside made of newspaper covered with fringes of crepe paper or rice paper.

In some families, the art of making parols is passed down from generation to generation. Everyone is involved. Beginning in July, the men and boys cut bamboo frames for the parols. By October, frames of many sizes and shapes have been completed. Cutting the paper sides of the parols and pasting them to the frames is completed by women and children. Parols are finished with a trim of lace doilies, foil cutouts, tassels, or fringed pom-poms.

All the parols are ready for sale by mid-November. Stalls are set up in front of homes, or shops are rented. Parols are displayed on overhead strings, crossing streets from shop to shop. They hang so low that they touch the heads of adults passing underneath. By mid-December all are sold.

The pageants, festivals, and music used in Christmas celebrations may have evolved from old tribal customs mixed with Chinese, Spanish, and American traditions. Serenading *cumbancheros*, or strolling minstrels, end their performances by singing *Maligayang Pasko* to the tune of "Happy Birthday." Cumbancheros use musical instruments made from coconut shells, carabao bones, split bamboo, and tin-can ends. These handmade banjos, castanets, tambourines, and cymbals are an important part of the sounds of Christmas in the Philippines.

Sweden

SYMBOL: *St. Lucia crown*
GREETING: God Jul, *or Good Yule*
WEATHER: *Dark winter days, with only a few hours of sun; snow may stay on the ground for over six months*

Sweden, the largest of the Scandinavian countries, is part of a peninsula shared by Norway. It is a land blanketed with forests and over 90,000 lakes. The capital city, Stockholm, includes twenty islands and peninsulas on the Baltic Sea. Most Swedish citizens live near water.

The first Sunday of Advent, four Sundays before Christmas, marks the beginning of the Christmas celebration in Sweden. Church services are well attended, and communities start to decorate streets and buildings with greenery and lights. Almost every home displays a four-candle Advent candelabra. On each of the Sundays of Advent, a candle is lit. Swedish children also count the days until Christmas with an Advent calendar. These calendars show a Christmas scene with twenty-five numbered "windows." Every morning, from December 1 through December 25, a window is opened, revealing a cheerful symbol of the Christmas season painted underneath.

Through the long winter months the few hours of sunlight each day become Swedish treasures. This is certainly good reason to honor St. Lucia, the patron saint of light. The celebration of Lucia morning falls on December 13. This day, according to folk tradition, follows the longest night of the year.

On Lucia morning almost all Swedish homes, offices, and schools choose a "Lucia." These Lucias dress in long white gowns, each tied at the waist with a red ribbon. Their hair may be sprinkled with glitter, which catches the light from the crown of candles they wear. This custom honors an old legend in which St. Lucia appears, her head encircled in light, bringing food during a terrible famine. Boys are also dressed in white, but instead of candles they wear tall cone-shaped paper hats covered with stars. The white-gowned boys and girls sing Lucia carols as they serve coffee and *lussekatter*, pinwheel-shaped saffron rolls, or ginger biscuits.

Christmas trees are usually brought into Swedish homes one or two days before Christmas. Decorations may include candles, apples, Swedish flags, small gnomes wearing red tasseled caps, and straw ornaments. The house may be filled with red tulips and the smell of *pepparkakor*, which is a heart-, star-, or goat-shaped gingerbread biscuit.

Swedish *Julafton*, or Christmas Eve, dinner may be a *smörgasbord*, or buffet, with *julskinka*, or Christmas ham; pickled pigs' feet; *lutfisk*, or dried codfish; and many different kinds of sweets. *Risgrynsgröt*, a special rice porridge, is served hot with sprinkles of cinnamon and sugar. Hidden in the porridge is a single almond. Tradition has it that whoever finds the almond in his or her bowl will marry in the coming year.

After Christmas Eve dinner a friend or family member dresses up as the *tomte*, or Christmas gnome. The tomte, unlike Santa Claus, is supposed to live under the floorboards of the house or barn and ride a straw goat. The make-believe tomte, wearing a white beard and dressed in red robes, distributes gifts from his sack. Many are given with a funny rhyme that hints at the contents.

The Christmas season ends on *Tjugondag Knut*, or St. Knut's Day, which is January 13, a week after Epiphany. St. Knut ruled as King Knut IV from 1080–1086 and was known for his generosity toward the poor. During this final holiday party, adults carefully remove fragile ornaments from the Christmas tree while children and their friends remove all edible decorations. The tree is then tossed out of the house as they sing this song:

> *Christmas has come to an end,*
> *And the tree must go.*
> *But the next year once again*
> *We shall see our dear old friend,*
> *For he has promised us so.*

United States *Alaska*

SYMBOL: *Tinsel-trimmed wheels, called stars*
GREETING: Hriztos razhdaetsya, *or Christ is born!*
WEATHER: *Rare December sunlight, dominated by rain and snow*

The word *Alaska* is from the language of a native American people, the Aleuts. Defined many ways, it can mean "land that is not an island," "that which the sea breaks against," or "great land." Alaska is so big that if it were placed on top of the continental forty-eight states (Alaska is the forty-ninth), it would stretch from the Carolinas to California. Alaska's coastline is longer than the coastlines of all the other states combined, with a total length of 6,640 miles. The land is also sparsely settled. There are twenty cities in the continental United States with larger populations than that of the entire state of Alaska.

The most western of Alaska's Aleutian Islands stretches far into the Pacific Ocean, almost touching the Russian Federation peninsula of Kamchatka. Russian trappers settled on Kodiak Island long before 1867, when the United States paid Russia 7.2 million dollars to purchase the vast Alaska territory. The trappers brought with them the customs of their Russian Orthodox heritage. Most Christian Alaskans celebrate Christmas on December 25, just as people do in the continental United States. Santa Claus may arrive for a pre-Christmas visit via a United States Coast Guard ship, but food, gift giving, and decorations are like what you might see in Texas or Wisconsin.

Descendants of Russian settlers on Kodiak, however, still follow the calendar of the Russian Orthodox Church, which places Christmas on January 7. Their Christmas celebration often includes a procession called Carrying the Star. For three nights, beginning on January 7, men, women, and children move from house to house over icy roads, carrying tinsel-trimmed wheels, called stars.

Nowadays someone with a flashlight usually leads the way. However, in years past a *lampada*, or hanging lamp of candlelight, was the source of light.

The star bearers represent the angels who came to earth to announce the birth of Christ. The elaborate eight-point stars, almost as large as umbrellas, often have center decorations picturing angels or the Nativity scene. There may also be glass inserts decorated with flowers, miniature lights, and tinsel. Many of the stars have parts that are over one hundred years old. Each family repaints and restores its star each year.

In the city of Old Harbor on Kodiak Island, this custom is known by its Slavonic Russian name, *Slavek*, or glory. The ritual begins at the church. The church icon, a painting of a religious image, is saluted with Russian Orthodox hymns or old Aleut songs. The group of carolers then sets out. At each home, lights inside the house are dimmed as carolers gather around the family's icon, singing Christmas carols in Slavonic and Aleut.

The songs sung at each home usually include the Aleut words *Gřistuusaaq suu'uq*, or "Christ is born." Twirling the stars represents transmission of holy messages contained in the carols. Everyone joins in the closing words, *Mnogaya leta*, or "God grant you many years." At the conclusion of the caroling the host provides carolers with maple-frosted doughnuts, cookies, candy, *piřuk*, or fish pie, and sometimes smoked salmon.

The state flag of Alaska, designed by a thirteen-year-old schoolboy, has seven gold stars, which represent the Big Dipper. An eighth star in the upper corner is symbolic of Alaska's location in the Far North.

Christmas Crafts
by Irene Norman

Be sure to have an adult close by to help with the cutting, gluing, and *especially* the cooking and ironing called for to make these projects. Never use the stove or an iron by yourself!

Pinecone Pine Trees

Pinecones contain seeds from evergreen trees, like the ones grown in Canada for Christmas celebrations in other parts of the world. Make these miniature Christmas trees as gifts or holiday decorations.

Materials

    pinecones
    rye-grass seed
    tuna fish cans or plastic
      butter tubs
    sand
    paint, contact paper, or
      ribbon

Your pinecones will look like miniature Christmas trees, with grass that resembles pine needles, ten days after you start this project.

1. Soak pinecones in water overnight. Decorate tuna cans or butter tubs with paint, contact paper, or ribbon.

2. Fill tuna cans or butter tubs with sand, and bury pinecones deeply enough that they stand upright.

3. Sprinkle grass seeds between petals of cones while they are wet.

4. Keep sand wet and, each day, sprinkle cones with water. Grass will sprout in a few days.

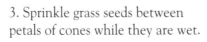

Nativity Scenes

*F*rom Guatemala to Italy, people all over the world treasure their nativity scenes. You can make your own—as simple or as elaborate as you wish—by creating these figures from the Christmas story.

Materials

self-hardening clay (see recipes—either is good for this project) or Play-doh or Crayola Model Magic
aluminum foil, waxed paper, or breadboard
food coloring
saucepan
rolling pin
wooden spoon

Salt and Flour Clay

1 cup salt
1 cup flour
1 tablespoon powdered alum (available from supermarkets and drugstores)

Mix with enough water to form a thick putty.

Cornstarch and Baking-soda Clay

1 cup cornstarch
2 cups baking soda
1¼ cups water

Combine all materials in a saucepan. Cook over medium heat, stirring all the time. When mixture thickens, turn it out on the foil, waxed paper, or breadboard. Let cool. (Food coloring may be added when cool enough.)

*S*tore the clay in plastic bags to keep it soft. When you're ready, shape it into figures of Mary, Joseph, and Baby Jesus. Try angels, Wise Men, shepherds, sheep, camels, cows—any creature that pleases you. A simple manger can be made from a cardboard box.

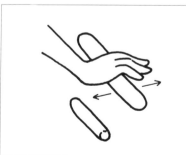

1. To make the arms, legs, and bodies of your manger characters, roll out clay in cylinders. To shape the body, stand one cylinder on end.

2. Pinch a spot about three-quarters of the way up the body for the neck. The section of the cylinder above the pinch will be the head.

3. Roll out a flat sheet of clay for a robe to wrap around the figures.

Stars

In the Philippines, the art of making parols is handed down from generation to generation. You can make your own star to celebrate the light that guided the Wise Men to Bethlehem.

Materials

waxed paper
paper, or other material for making stars
crayons
crayon sharpener
newspaper
iron and ironing board
glue or tape
thread, string, or ribbon
scissors

You can use all kinds of material—including Christmas wrapping paper and aluminum foil—to make stars. See what you can think of to use. When you've made your stars, carefully poke a small hole in the top of each one with the point of the scissors, and hang with thread, string, or ribbon.

Waxed-paper Star

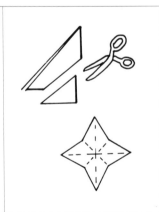

Cut two stars out of waxed paper. Put crayon shavings between them. Place stars between four or five sheets of old newspapers. Iron the layers of newspaper to melt the crayon wax.

Four-Point Star

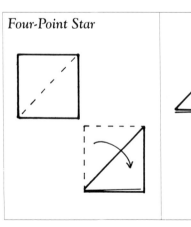

1. Fold a square sheet of paper into a triangle.

2. Make a second fold, then a third.

3. Cut a wedge, as shown; unfold wedge to find star.

Five-Point Star

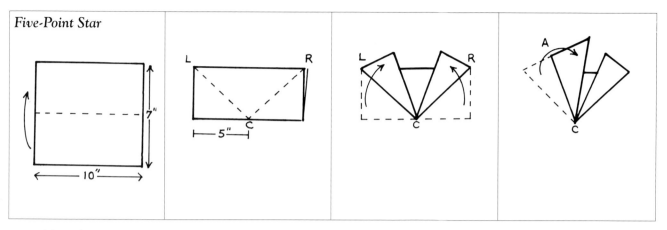

1. Fold a 7-by-10-inch piece of paper in half lengthwise.

2. Fold along lines CL and CR.

3. Fold left-hand triangle along line CA.

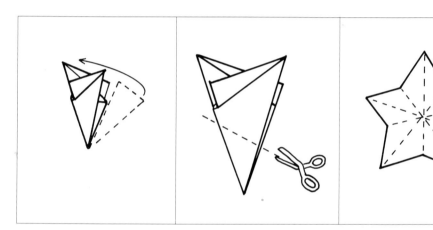

4. Fold right-hand triangle back, as shown.

5. Cut here.

6. Unfold the small piece to find your star.

After you've made your star, you may decide to decorate it. Try a splash of glitter, or give your star a tinsel tail! Backing your star with cardboard will make it stronger.

Six-Point Star

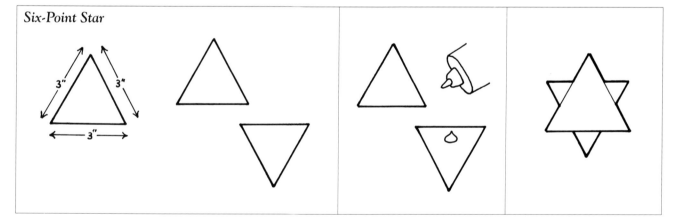

1. Cut two equilateral triangles out of paper (all three sides should have the same length).

2. Turn one triangle upside down and overlap the triangles, as shown.

3. Glue the triangles together.

Christmas Cards

*C*hristmas cards are even more special when made by hand. They can be religious, funny, dignified, or joyful, with your personal holiday message written inside.

Materials

- construction paper
- scrap materials (doilies, foil, nylon net, wallpaper, fabric, glitter, stickers)
- glue
- white tempera or poster paint
- toothbrush
- wire screen
- medium-sized shallow box
- scissors
- tape
- pencils, markers, or crayons

Cutaway Cards

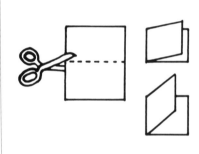

1. Cut construction paper in half. Fold each half sheet as a card.

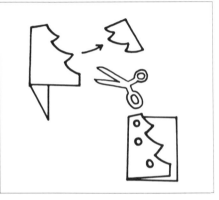

2. On the front, draw a Christmas symbol—a tree, wreath, or stocking, for instance—and then cut away the outer edge of the drawing. (Be sure not to cut near the fold of the card.)

Stenciled Cards

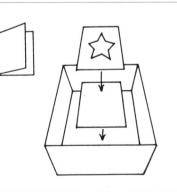

1. Make a stencil by drawing a simple, clear picture on construction paper and then cutting it out carefully.

2. Fold a piece of construction paper in half to use as a card. Place the stencil on top of the card. Put the card and stencil in a shallow, medium-sized box.

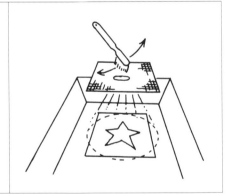

3. Mix paint. Apply a little paint to the toothbrush, then carefully brush back and forth over the wire screen. Paint will spatter through the screen onto the stencil and card.

Collage Cards

1. Cut out fabric or other scrap materials in Christmas shapes.

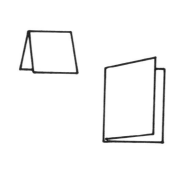

2. Fold a piece of construction paper in half to make a card.

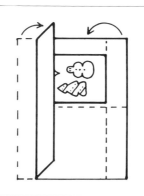

3. Glue the fabric on the front of the card.

Envelopes

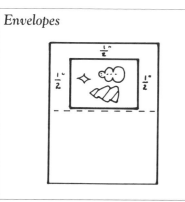

1. Fold a piece of paper in half. Make sure paper is ½ inch larger than your card at left, top, and right.

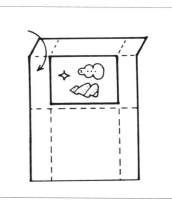

2. Fold left and right flaps over card. Crease sides so they lie flat, then unfold.

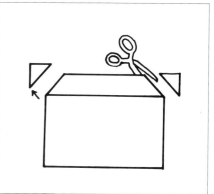

3. Fold top flap over card. Crease along edge so it will lie flat, then unfold.

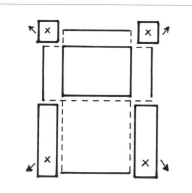

4. Remove areas marked by Xs by cutting along the creased lines.

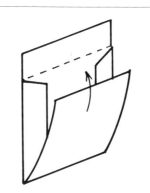

5. Fold all flaps onto card. Start with sides, then fold the bottom flap up.

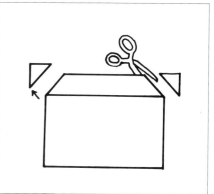

6. Cut out small triangles on top flap and fold flap over. Seal envelope with tape.

Christmas Cornucopias

*C*ornucopias, overflowing with goodies, capture all the bounty of the holiday season. Use them to decorate a Christmas tree or hang them outdoors, as a "thank-you" to the birds who stay in winter.

*W*hat are some fun things you can use to fill the cornucopias? You could try candy, nuts, coins, or small toys. Fill your outdoor ornaments with birdseed.

Materials

Christmas wrapping paper or tagboard
tape or glue
ribbon or yarn
    for hanging
ruler

Circular Cones

 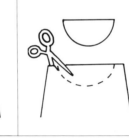 

1. Trace halfway around a bowl or small plate to get a half-circle shape.

2. Cut out the half-circle.

3. Bend the half-circle into a cone until the two straight edges overlap. Tape the edges.

4. You can vary the basic cone as shown.

Wedge-shaped Cones

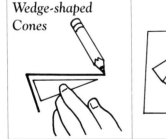 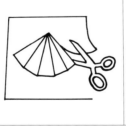 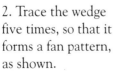 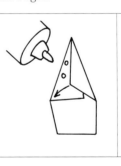

1. Try thin wedge patterns cut out of tagboard.

2. Trace the wedge five times, so that it forms a fan pattern, as shown.

3. Cut out the fan and fold it on the lines, using a ruler to make the folds crisp.

4. Overlap two of the wedges and tape or glue them together so that the finished cornucopia has four sides.

5. Cut a strip of tagboard and glue it on as a handle. Hang the ornament with ribbon or yarn.

Christmas Party Crackers

elebrate as the British do by putting these festive favors on your holiday table. They also make intriguing Christmas tree ornaments and stocking stuffers—with a surprise inside!

Materials

Christmas wrapping paper
paper towel tubes
string or ribbon
small toys or other small favors
scissors

an you think of unusual small trinkets to surprise your friends and family with? You might write a fortune or wishes for the New Year, or wrap pennies, candy, or grapes. What else can you find?

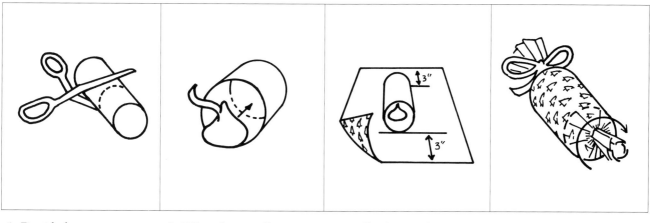

1. Decide how many crackers you want to make, and then cut tubes into equal lengths.

2. Fill with a small toy or other favor.

3. Roll tube in Christmas wrapping paper large enough to lap over each end at least 3 inches. Do not use tape or glue.

4. Twist the paper at the ends to seal the cracker or tie it with string or ribbon.

Advent Calendars

*C*hildren in Sweden and many other countries count the days to Christmas by opening the little doors on their Advent calendars.

*D*ecide what kind of Advent calendar you want to make. Plan your drawing on newsprint or butcher paper before you make your final drawing on good paper.

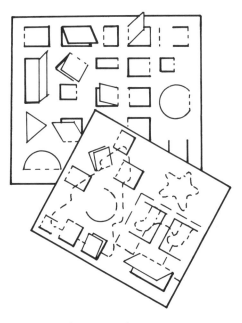

Materials

> drawing paper, newsprint, or butcher paper
> poster board or tagboard
> pictures from catalogs
> holiday stickers or decorative stamps
> glue
> crayons, colored pencils, map pencils,
>   or markers
> scissors, or craft or utility knife

The most traditional Advent calendars have twenty-four doors; #1 is opened on December 1, and a new door is opened every day until Christmas. If this is your choice, then plan out a Christmas scene with enough room for twenty-four doors, windows, or flaps. It could show a large Christmas tree with packages piled underneath, or a store window just waiting to be "decorated."

Try a winter night with clouds and stars, or a scene with Santa Claus in his sleigh flying over a chimney top. What else can you think of?

How about a luggage claim section at an airport, with flaps on each suitcase or pet-carrying case?

You might enjoy making a "Twelve Days of Christmas" calendar, with flaps to open from December 25 through Epiphany, January 6, which is also called Twelfth Night or Three Kings Day. These twelve days celebrate the journey of the Wise Men to Jesus' birthplace in Bethlehem. What kinds of scenes could you plan for a calendar like this?

1. Draw your final picture on good paper.

2. Cut open the flaps, or "doors."

3. Then match the picture up with a piece of poster board that's exactly the same size. Lift the flaps and lightly draw a box on the poster board to mark the position of each opening, so you will know how big your hidden pictures should be, and where they go.

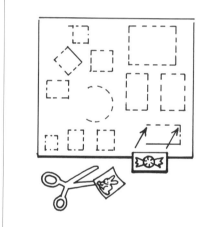

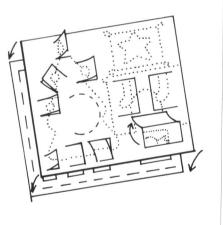

4. Paste the catalog pictures in the boxes on the poster board.

5. After the glue is dry, paste the original picture on the poster board, making sure that the catalog cutouts align under the flaps.

6. Then close the flaps and glue the picture to the poster board with a line of glue on all four sides.

𝒥rene Norman, formerly art consultant for the Irving, Texas, Independent School District, has worked with countless children to create craft projects that are entertaining to make, decorative, and useful, and that require only easily available materials. She hopes making these crafts will help readers celebrate Christmas in a noncommercial way and that they will use her ideas to inspire original ideas of their own!

Fact and Fiction

Advent: Beginning the fourth Sunday before Christmas, the days that follow are designated as Advent, or the Season of the Coming. Advent ends Christmas Eve at midnight.

Anno Domini: This Latin phrase means "in the year of our Lord." It is usually abbreviated as A.D. and designates passage of time since the birth of Christ. Dionysius Exiguus, a Scythian monk, is credited with the idea of dividing history into two eras: B.C., or the years before the birth of Christ, and A.D., the years following the birth.

Auld lang syne: These Scottish words, which mean "good old days" or "time remembered with fondness," are from a song usually sung at Christmas or on the eve of the new year.

Candles: Consider a world in which the only source of light was the small flame flickering atop a candle. Candles were symbolic of the pagan hope that longer days of sunlight would return following dark winter days. Candles are used in religious rites to celebrate Jesus as the "Light of the World."

Carols: These simple, joyful songs celebrate Christmas. St. Francis of Assisi introduced carols to formal church services.

Chimney: Many gift-giving traditions are associated with chimneys. Hanging stockings from the mantel may have originated with the legend of St. Nicholas, who was said to have thrown bags of gold down a chimney into stockings hung up to dry.

Christians: The Christian belief is based on the Bible and on the acceptance of Jesus as the Son of God. Christianity was founded in the first century in Palestine by disciples of Jesus. An estimated one billion people belong to Catholic, Protestant, and Eastern Orthodox congregations.

Christmas: Telesphorus, the second bishop of Rome, A.D. 125–c. 136, declared that public church services should be held to celebrate the "Nativity of our Lord and Savior." By A.D. 320, Pope Julius I and other religious leaders specified December 25 as the official date of the birth of Christ.

Epiphany, or Twelfth Night: Falling on January 6, Epiphany comes from the Greek word for *showing*. It celebrates the day when the Christ Child was shown to the Magi, who brought gifts of gold, frankincense, and myrrh.

Gift givers: *St. Nicholas*, born in A.D. 280 in Patara, a city of Lycia in Asia Minor, became the bishop of Myra. His Christmas gifts were given late at night, so that the gift giver's identity would remain a secret. St. Nicholas was eventually named the patron saint of children, sailors, Russia, and Greece. *Kris Kringle* evolved from the German name for the Christ Child, *Christkindlein*. *Père Noël* is the French term for Father Christmas. French children also receive gifts from *le Petit Noël*, or Little Christmas. Russian children expect gifts from *Baboushka* during the night of January 5. In Brazil, *Papa Noël* arrives on Christmas Eve. Dutch settlers in New Amsterdam, which became New York, changed St. Nicholas to *Sinta Claes*. This name eventually became *Santa Claus*.

Jesus Christ: The name *Jesus* is Greek for the Hebrew word *Joshua*, which means "Savior." *Christos* is the Greek word for the Hebrew *Messiah*, which means "anointed."

Magi: The plural of *magus*, a Latin word that means

"magician," or member of a group of ancient priests. Also known as Wise Men of the East, from the biblical verse "…there came wise men from the east to Jerusalem" (Matthew 2:1).

Manger scenes: St. Francis of Assisi began the practice of using figures to re-create the Nativity scene. These scenes depict Mary, Joseph, the Christ Child, and others present in the stable where Christ was born. The manger scene is called crèche, or cradle (France); *Krippe*, or crib (Germany); *presepio*, or manger (Italy); *nacimiento*, or Nativity scene (Mexico, Guatemala).

Mummer: This word also means "masker" and is used for any person who masquerades as someone else in a parade, play, or pageant. In ancient Rome, during the festival called *Saturnalia*, people dressed in costume. Men would wear women's clothing or animal costumes, and everyone enjoyed making loud music and creating disruptions. This tradition continued in various forms through the ages. In the United States the Philadelphia Mummers' Parade is over one hundred years old.

Noel: Some of the oldest carols were French *noëls*. This word is probably from the Latin word *natalis*, or "birthday." *Noel* is also used to describe the Christmas season.

Pagan: In Latin, a pagan was a worshiper of false gods, a civilian, or "not a soldier of Christ." We usually think of pagans as ancient people whose beliefs were based on their explanations for natural events that affected their lives.

Saturnalia: A season of riotous celebration in ancient Rome, from December 17 to 24, honoring Saturn, the god of agriculture. Less excessive festivities included the exchange of gifts of cakes and fruits, decoration of homes, and celebrations with singing and candles. These ancient rites form the basis for many Christian customs.

Wassail: A toast, from the Anglo-Saxon words *waes hael*, which translates as "to your health," "what hail," "here's to you," or "be whole." Wassail was also a hot drink, a mixture of wine or ale, eggs, sugar, nutmeg, cloves, ginger, and roasted apples. It was usually served in a bowl with pieces of toast floating on top. Words spoken as a tribute when drinking are now called a "toast." Originally, apple trees were sprinkled with wassail to ensure a good crop. The old custom of carrying a wooden wassail bowl from home to home evolved into the tradition of caroling parties whose singers are invited inside for a cup of fruitlike punch, or wassail.

Winter solstice: *Solstice* is the Latin term for "sun standing still." Winter solstice is the date, usually December 22, when the sun is at its greatest distance from the equator. It is the shortest day of the year in the Northern Hemisphere. Ancient people, with little understanding of science, believed the sun stood still during the short winter days. They turned to fire and its warmth as symbolic of spring and their hope for the return of longer hours of sunlight.

Xmas: An abbreviation of the word *Christmas*. The letter X is the Greek letter *Chi*, the first letter of Christ's name written in the Greek alphabet.

Yule: Spelled in Old English as *geol, houl, hioul*, and in Norse as *jul*, this word was used to describe pagan midwinter festivals in honor of the sun. Yule logs were burned during these rites for protection against evil spirits and to destroy old misunderstandings and hatreds. To ensure the sun's continued warmth, a part of the log was saved to light the yule log the following year. Today the word *yule* is frequently used to describe the Christmas season, although the only log seen at Christmas may be the *bûche de Noël*, a traditional French log-shaped cake.

Pronunciation Guide

aulein   oh-lihn

Babbo Natale   BAH-boh nah-TAH-lay

Bambino Gesù   bahm-BEE-noh jay-ZHOO

Befana   beh-FAH-nah

boulettes   boo-LEHT

buñuelos   boo-NYWAY-lohs

Buon Natale   bwohn nah-TAH-lay

ceppo   SEH-poh

chirimias   chee-ree-MEE-ahs

choraulein   khoh-roh-lihn

Christkindlein   krist-KIN-tlihn

Christkindlesmarkt   krist-KIN-tuhls-mahrkt

Christopsomo   hrees-TOH-psoh-moh

cosaques   koh-sack

cumbancheros   kuhm-bahn-CHEHR-ohs

dabtaras   dab-tahr-och

el Dia de la Candelaria   ehl DEE-yah day lah kahn-deh-
            LAHR-ee-uh

el Dia de los Reyes   ehl DEE-yah day lohs RAY-ehs

ensalada de la noche buena   ehn-sah-LAH-dah day lah
            NOH-cheh boo-AY-nuh

ensalada navideña   ehn-sah-LAH-dah nah-vee-DAY-nyah

Feliz Navidad   fay-LEEZ nah-vee-DAHD

flor de la noche buena   flor day lah NOH-cheh boo-AY-nuh

Fröhliche Weihnachten   FROY-likh-eh vy-NAHCK-tehn

Ganna   guh-nah

God Jul   gudt yool

Gřistuusaaq suu'uq   kris-TOO-suck SOO-ok

Heiligabend   HIGH-likh-ar-bernt

Hriztos razhdaetsya   hris-TAWS rah-DEES-yah

Hronia polla   hroh-nee-yah poh-LAH

injerá   in-jehr-uh

Joyeux Noël   zhwah-YUH noh-EL

Julafton   yool-AHF-ton

julskinka   yool-SHIN-kah

Kala Christougena   KAH-lah hrees-TOO-yen-ah

Klöpfelnachten   KLOH-pfehl-nahckt-en

kourambiethes   koo-rahm-BEETH-ehs

la Noche de los Rábanos   lah NOH-cheh day lohs
            RAH-bah-noass

las posadas   lahs poh-SAH-dahs

lebkuchen   LEHB-koo-kehn

lussekatter   LOOH-sah-KAH-tor

lutfisk   loot-fisk

makamiya   mah-koh-mee-yah

Maligayang Pasko   mal-ee-gay-yang PAHS-koh

meleket   meh-leh-kuht

Melkm Ganna   mel-kuhm guh-nah

Misa de Gallo   MEE-sah deh GAH-yoh

Mnogaya leta   m-NO-ga-ya LYEH-ta

nacimiento   nah-see-mee-EHN-toh

Palo Voladare   PAH-low voh-lah-DAH-ray

panettone   pah-neh-TOH-neh

Panunuluyan   PAHN-uh-loo-yahn

parol   pah-ROHL

pastore   pah-STOR-eh

pecorino   peh-kor-EEN-oh

pefanino   pay-fah-NEE-noh

pepparkakor   PEH-pahr-kaa-koor

piñata   peen-YAH-tuh

praesaepe   pray-see-pay

presepi   pray-SEH-pee

presepio   pray-SEH-pee-oh

puestos   PWEHS-tohs

puto bumbong   poo-toh boom-bong

réveillon   rehv-ay-YON

Reyes Magos   RAY-es MAH-gohs

risgrynsgröt   rees-grewns-grurt

rolyo   roll-yoh

shamma   shuh-mah

sistrum   sees-trum

Tannenbaum   TAH-nuhn-bowm

Timkat   tim-kuht

Tjugondag Knut   chew-GAHN-dahg can-ewt

tomte   TAWM-teh

tourtière   tor-tee-AIR

Tres Reyes   trace RAY-ehs

weisse wochen   VIGH-seh vo-khen

yeferas guks   yeh-fehr-uhs gooks

zampognari   zahm-pawg-NAH-ree

Zwetschgenfrauen   tsvehsh-gehn-FROW-ern

Zwetschgenmännla   tsvehsh-gehn-MAHN-lah

Christmas Sayings

Christmas superstitions were often used to explain natural phenomena and interpret events of the winter months. It is difficult to trace the origins of these sayings to an exact time or place. As part of an ancient folk heritage, they can be included in all our Christmas traditions. Write them on colored paper and tuck the papers inside homemade Christmas crackers, or use the sayings to decorate place cards at a festive meal. Christmas sayings make wonderful messages on cards and invitations, but they are also fun to think about and say out loud, remembering that long ago people celebrated Christmas in a world very different from our own.

On Christmas Eve all animals can speak. However, it is bad luck to test this superstition.

The child born on Christmas Day will have a special fortune.

Good luck will come to the home where a fire is kept burning throughout the Christmas season.

To have good health throughout the next year, eat an apple on Christmas Eve.

Snow on Christmas means Easter will be green.

Eat plum pudding on Christmas and avoid losing a friend before next Christmas.

Shout "Christmas gift" to the first person knocking on your door on Christmas Day and expect to receive a gift from the visitor.

Place shoes side by side on Christmas Eve to prevent a quarreling family.

Wearing new shoes on Christmas Day will bring bad luck.

A clear star-filled sky on Christmas Eve will bring good crops in the summer.

A blowing wind on Christmas Day brings good luck.

Bibliography

Barth, Edna. *Christmas Feast: Poems, Sayings, Greetings, and Wishes.* Boston: Clarion Books, Houghton Mifflin Co., 1979.

——. *Holly, Reindeer, and Colored Lights: The Story of Christmas Symbols.* Boston: Clarion Books, Houghton Mifflin Co., 1971.

Christmas in Mexico. Chicago: World Book Encyclopedia, Inc., 1976.

Cosman, Madeleine Pelner. *Medieval Holidays and Festivals, a Calendar of Celebrations.* New York: Charles Scribner's Sons, 1981.

Del Re, Gerald, and Patricia Del Re. *Christmas Almanack.* New York: Doubleday Publishing Co., 1979.

Dobler, Lavinia. *Customs and Holidays Around the World.* New York: Fleet Press Corporation, 1962.

Downman, Lorna, Paul Britten Austin, and Anthony Baird. *Round the Swedish Year: Daily Life and Festivals Through Four Seasons.* Stockholm: The Swedish Institute, 1967.

Foley, Daniel J. *Christmas the World Over: How the Season of Joy and Good Will Is Observed and Enjoyed by Peoples Here and Everywhere.* Radnor, Pennsylvania: Chilton Book Company, 1963.

Hottes, Alfred Carl. *1001 Christmas Facts and Fancies.* New York: Dodd, Mead & Company, 1937.

Ingeborg, Relph, and Penny Stanway. *Christmas, a Cook's Tour.* Oxford, England: A Lion Book, 1991.

Knightly, Charles. *The Customs and Ceremonies of Britain, an Encyclopaedia of Living Traditions.* London: Thames and Hudson Ltd., 1986.

Liman, Ingemar. *Traditional Festivities in Sweden.* Stockholm: The Swedish Institute, 1983.

MacDonald, Margaret Read, editor. *The Folklore of World Holidays.* Detroit, Michigan: Gale Research, Inc., 1992.

Megas, George A. *Greek Calendar Customs.* Athens: Press and Information Department, Prime Minister's Office, 1958.

Murkowski, Carol. "Stars Over Old Harbor." *Alaska* 56 (no. 1), January 1990.

Peitzsch, Inge. *Make the Most of Life, G'lebt is glei: Bavarian Festivities, Bavarian Customs,* trans. Sandy A. Pirie. West Germany: Weidling Vertag GmbH, 1981.

Pettersen, Carmen L. *Maya of/de Guatemala, Life and Dress/Vida y Traje.* Guatemala City: Ixchel Museum, 1976.

Reekie, Jennie. *The London Ritz Book of Christmas.* New York: William Morrow and Company, Inc., 1989.

Russ, Jennifer M. *German Festivals and Customs.* London: Oswald Wolff, 1982.

Smith, Jeff. *The Frugal Gourmet Celebrates Christmas.* New York: William Morrow and Company, Inc., 1991.

Van Straalen, Alice. *The Book of Holidays Around the World.* New York: E. P. Dutton, 1986.

Wernecke, Herbert H. *Christmas Customs Around the World.* Philadelphia: The Westminster Press, 1973.

Index

The traditional verse "Befana, Befana," on page 23, is reprinted courtesy of the Folklore Society
(Gower Street, London, England); the traditional verse "Christmas Has Come to an End," on page 28,
was found in *Christmas, A Cook's Tour,* by Relph Ingeborg and Penny Stanway
(Lion Publishing, Oxford, England).

Watercolor, gouache, and colored pencils on 140 Fabriano watercolor paper were used for the full-color illustrations.
The text type is 12-point Goudy Old Style.

Text copyright © 1995 by Mary D. Lankford
Illustrations copyright © 1995 by Karen Dugan

Printed in Singapore at Tien Wah Press.

6 7 8 9 10

Library of Congress Cataloging-in-Publication Data
Lankford, Mary D.   Christmas around the world/Mary D. Lankford; illustrated by Karen Dugan   p.   cm.
Includes bibliographical references and index.
ISBN 0-688-12166-7 (trade)—ISBN 0-688-12167-5 (library)
1. Christmas—Juvenile literature.   [1. Christmas]   I. Dugan, Karen, ill.   II. Title.   GT4985.5.L36   1994
394.2'663—dc20   93-38566   CIP   AC